SOLOS
for the
TROMBONE
PLAYER

With Piano Accompaniment

Selected and Edited by

HENRY C. SMITH

ED. 2477

G. SCHIRMER, Inc.

DISTRIBUTED BY
HAL•LEONARD®
CORPORATION
7777 W. BLUEMOUND RD. P.O. BOX 13819 MILWAUKEE, WI 53213

Foreword

Amateur and professional trombonists often have difficulty in finding solo repertoire of the highest musical quality. Most composers of recent centuries have written little for the trombone as a solo instrument. Therefore several transcriptions are included in this volume as well as original works for trombone.

Of particular interest is the *Andante* movement of an excellent *Sonatina for Trombone and Piano* by Kazimierz Serocki, who lives in Warsaw, Poland. The unaccompanied *Elegy for Mippy II,* by Leonard Bernstein, is a novel and welcome addition to the trombonist's solo repertoire.

H.C.S.

CONTENTS

The two movements from Sonatas by Johann Ernst Galliard published in this collection are from Johann Ernst Galliard *Six Sonatas for Bassoon and figured bass*, arranged for trombone and piano by John Clark, figured bass set by Edith Weiss-Mann, published by McGinnis & Marx, New York.
Reprinted by permission.

III

Index by Composers

1

1. Preludio

from: Violin Sonata in F

Arcangelo Corelli (1653-1713)

Adagio

Trombone

Piano

2. Alla Siciliano

from: Sonata V for Bassoon

Johann Ernst Galliard (1687-1749)

3. Menuet alternat

from: Sonata VI for Bassoon

Johann Ernst Galliard

4. Sarabande

from: Oboe Concerto in G Minor

George Frideric Handel (1685-1759)

6

45202

5. Adagio cantabile

from: Sonata VI for Violin

George Frideric Handel

6. Chorale

from: Sleepers, Wake!

Johann Sebastian Bach (1685-1750)

10

45202

12

7. Arioso

from: Piano Concerto in F Minor

Johann Sebastian Bach

8. Adagio

from: Concerto for Cello and Orchestra

Joseph Haydn (1732-1809)

45202

9. Recitative and Prayer

from: Grand Symphony for Band, Op. 15

Hector Berlioz (1803-1869)

SOLOS
for the
TROMBONE
PLAYER

With Piano Accompaniment

Selected and Edited by
HENRY C. SMITH

ED. 2477

G. SCHIRMER, *Inc.*

DISTRIBUTED BY
HAL•LEONARD®
CORPORATION
7777 W. BLUEMOUND RD. P.O. BOX 13819 MILWAUKEE, WI 53213

Foreword

Amateur and professional trombonists often have difficulty in finding solo repertoire of the highest musical quality. Most composers of recent centuries have written little for the trombone as a solo instrument. Therefore several transcriptions are included in this volume as well as original works for trombone.

Of particular interest is the *Andante* movement of an excellent *Sonatina for Trombone and Piano* by Kazimierz Serocki, who lives in Warsaw, Poland. The unaccompanied *Elegy for Mippy II,* by Leonard Bernstein, is a novel and welcome addition to the trombonist's solo repertoire.

H.C.S.

The player should mark each selection with these cue markings for ease of use. To include as many selections as possible on the record, it was necessary to eliminate certain repeats. Listen to the record and mark the music accordingly before playing with the record.

1. Preludio - Corelli	Adagio	4 taps (1 measure) precede music.
2. Alla Siciliano - Galliard	Andantino	5 taps plus 1 silent (1 meas.) precede music.
3. Menuet alternat - Galliard	Tempo di menuetto	
		3 taps (1 measure) precede music.
5. Adagio cantabile - G. F. Handel	Adagio cant.	4 taps (1 measure) precede music.
7. Arioso - J. S. Bach	Mod. cant.	4 taps (1 measure) precede music.
8. Adagio - Haydn		4 taps (1 measure) precede music.
13. Vocalise - Rachmaninoff		4 taps (1 measure) precede music.

CONTENTS

III

Index by Composers

TROMBONE

1. Preludio

from: Violin Sonata in F

Arcangelo Corelli (1653 - 1713)

45202 c

TROMBONE

2. Alla Siciliano

from: Sonata V for Bassoon

Johann Ernst Galliard (1687-1749)

3. Menuet alternat

from: Sonata VI for Bassoon

Johann Ernst Galliard

TROMBONE

4. Sarabande

from: Oboe Concerto in G Minor

George Frideric Handel (1685-1759)

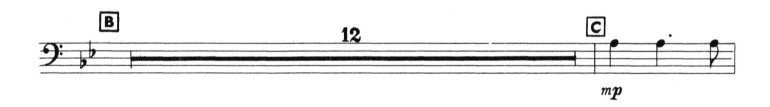

45202

5. Adagio cantabile

from: Sonata VI for Violin

TROMBONE

George Frideric Handel

6. Chorale

from: Sleepers, Wake!

Johann Sebastian Bach (1685-1750)

TROMBONE

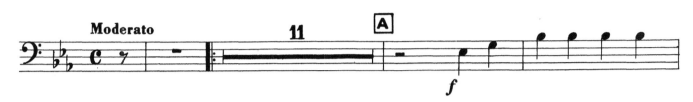

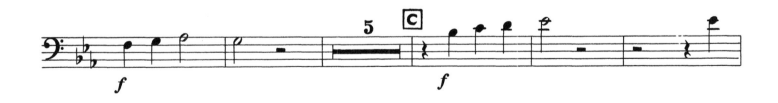

45202

TROMBONE

7. Arioso

from: Piano Concerto in F Minor

Johann Sebastian Bach

45202

TROMBONE

8. Adagio

from: Concerto for Cello and Orchestra

Joseph Haydn (1732-1809)

45202

9. Recitative and Prayer

from: Grand Symphony for Band, Op. 15

TROMBONE

Hector Berlioz (1803-1869)

10. Panis Angelicus

from: Messe Solennelle

César Franck (1822-1890)

TROMBONE

* *See piano accompaniment for antiphonal Trombone part.*

45202

11. Andante Cantabile

TROMBONE

from: Concerto for Trombone and Band

Nikolai Rimsky-Korsakov (1844-1908)

45202

12. Rondo

from: Concerto No. 2

Eugene Reiche

TROMBONE

13. Vocalise

TROMBONE

Sergei Rachmaninoff, Op. 34 No. 14
(1873 - 1943)

Lentamente e molto cantabile

14. Second Movement

from: Sonatina for Trombone and Piano

TROMBONE

Kazimierz Serocki (1922-   )

© MCMLV, by Polskie Wydawnictwo Muzyczne

15. Concert Piece

TROMBONE

Alexandre Guilmant, Op. 88
(1837-1911)

16. Elegy for Mippy II*

for Trombone alone

TROMBONE *

Leonard Bernstein (1918-   )

* Mippy was a mongrel belonging to my brother Burtie.
** The trombonist should accompany himself by tapping one foot, *mf,* four to the bar, e.g.

45202

10. Panis Angelicus

from: Messe Solennelle

César Franck (1822-1890)

* Optional antiphonal trombone part beginning 6 measures after B

45202

26

45202

*Antiphonal trombone may play this line an octave lower.
45202

28

11. Andante Cantabile

from: Concerto for Trombone and Band

Nikolai Rimsky-Korsakov (1844-1908)

12. Rondo

from: Concerto No. 2

Eugene Reiche

13. Vocalise

Sergei Rachmaninoff, Op. 34 No. 14
(1873 - 1943)

Lentamente e molto cantabile

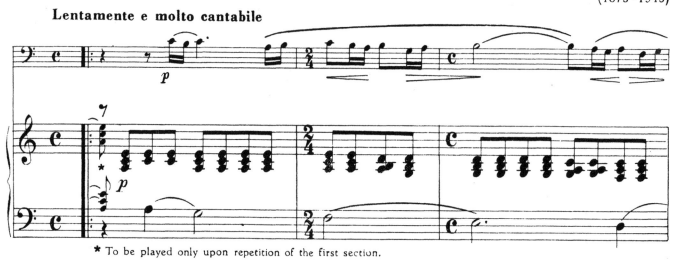

* To be played only upon repetition of the first section.

14. Second Movement

from: Sonatina for Trombone and Piano

Kazimierz Serocki (1922-   )

45202

Used by permission

15. Concert Piece

Alexandre Guilmant, Op. 88
(1837-1911)

cadenza ad lib.

rall.

p

Allegro moderato ♩ = 104

ff

mf

cresc.

mf

cresc.

f

f

45202